HOW OUR BODIES WORK
THE LUNGS AND BREATHING

MARK LAMBERT

Editorial planning
Philip Steele

SILVER BURDETT PRESS

Copyright © 1988 by Schoolhouse Press, Inc.
an imprint of Silver Burdett Press Inc.
Prentice Hall Building, Route 9W,
Englewood Cliffs, N.J. 07632

Original copyright, © Macmillan Education Limited 1988
© BLA Publishing Limited 1988

Designed and produced by BLA Publishing Limited,
Swan Court, East Grinstead, Sussex, England.

A Ling Kee Company

Illustrations by David Gifford, Anna Hancock, Sallie Alane
Reason
Color origination by Chris Willcock Reproductions
Printed in Hong Kong

94 95 96 10 9 8 7 6 5 4 3

Library of Congress Cataloging-in-Publication Data

Lambert, Mark, 1946–
    The lungs and breathing.

    (How our bodies work)
    Includes index.
    Summary: Describes the organs of the respiratory system and
their functions and discusses the consequences of disease and
prolonged abuse on this vital system.
    1. Respiration — Juvenile literature. [1. Respiratory
system] I. Title. II. Series.
QP121.L25   1988   612'.2   88-517
ISBN 0-382-09701-7 (hardback)

Photographic credits

t = top b = bottom l = left r = right

cover: Science Photo Library

4 Frank Lane Picture Library; 5 Horace Dobbs; 6
Bridgeman Colour Library; 8 Ann Ronan Picture
Library; 9 National Gallery; 11*t* J. Allan Cash; 11*b*
ZEFA; 12, 13 Science Photo Library; 14, 15 Vision
International; 17*t* J. Allan Cash; 17*b* S. & R. Greenhill;
18*t*, 18*b* Science Photo Library; 23 Trevor Hill; 24*t*
Vision International; 24*b* Science Photo library; 25 Chris
Fairclough Picture Library; 26 S. & R. Greenhill;
27*t* Vision International; 27*b*, 28, 29 Science Photo
Library; 30*t* Vivien Fifield; 30*b* Frank Lane Picture
Agency; 31 S. & R. Greenhill; 32*t*, 32*b* Science Photo
Library; 33 Vision International; 34*l* Science Photo
Library; 34*r* Ann Ronan Picture Library; 35 Science
Photo Library; 36 J. Allan Cash; 38, 39*t* Sporting
Pictures; 39 ZEFA; 40*t* S. & R. Greenhill; 40*b* ZEFA;
41 Science Photo Library; 42*t* S. & R. Greenhill; 42*b*
Vision International; 43 Trevor Hill; 44, 45 Science
Photo Library

How To Use This Book:
This book has many useful features. For example, look at the table of contents. See how it describes
each section in the book. Find a section you want to read and turn to it.

Notice that the section is a "two-page spread." That is, it covers two facing pages. Now look at
the headings in the spread. Headings are useful when you want to locate specific information. Next,
look at a photograph, drawing, chart or map and find its caption. Captions give you additional
information. A chart or map may also have labels to help you.

Scan the spread for a word in **bold print**. If you cannot find one in this spread, find one in
another spread. Bold-print words are defined in the glossary at the end of the book. Find your
bold-print word in the glossary.

Now turn to the index at the end of the book. When you have a specific topic or subject to
research, look for it in the index. you will quickly know whether the topic is in the book.

We hope you will use the features in this book to help you learn about new and exciting things.

Contents

Introduction

The air around our planet is made up of a thin layer of **gases**. The most important of these gases is **oxygen**. All living things on the earth need oxygen. They need to take in, or breathe, oxygen in order to stay alive. Plants and animals that live on the land get the oxygen they need from the air. Water plants and water animals get their oxygen from the water.

Air and Living Creatures

Each kind of living creature gets oxygen in its own way. Small animals that live in water take in oxygen through their skins.

Larger water animals often have special **organs** in their bodies which take in oxygen. These organs are called **gills**. Gills have enough blood just below the skin so that oxygen passes easily from the water into the blood. Fishes, crabs, and sea snails breathe through their gills.

A land animal needs a different kind of organ in order to breathe. The breathing organ has a thin, moist surface which can stretch to change its shape. For an earthworm this organ is its skin. It stays moist because the earthworm lives in the moist earth.

▼ A bird of prey needs a huge amount of energy in order to hover over one spot. Birds must take oxygen into their lungs in order to fly. The movements of their wings help to force the air out again.

Other animals have special organs inside their bodies. Insects breathe through tiny holes in their sides called **spiracles**. The spiracles lead to tubes. These tubes carry the oxygen to all parts of the insects' bodies.

The Way We Breathe

Creatures like frogs and newts start their lives as tadpoles. They live in the water and breathe through gills. Adult frogs and newts live on land. They breathe through two organs inside their bodies. These organs are called **lungs**. Lungs have a moist lining which never dries out.

▲ A dolphin is not a fish, but a mammal like us. It cannot take oxygen directly from the water. It has lungs, and must come up to the surface to breathe air. It breathes out through the blowhole in its head.

Creatures like snakes and lizards also use lungs for breathing. Some animals which live in the sea, such as whales, use lungs to breathe, too.

Humans have a pair of lungs in the chest. In this book we will learn how our lungs work. We will find out how oxygen gets into our blood and what happens to it there. We will also learn how to take good care of our lungs.

Long Ago

▲ This painting by Michelangelo shows God creating the first man, Adam. Many religions tell how the first people were made when gods breathed life into them. People have always known that breathing is a sign of being alive.

In the past, people could not understand what air was. It was not solid like stone. It was not liquid like water. Air did not seem to be made of anything. People knew, of course, that nothing could live without air. If living creatures had no air to breathe, they died. Air was very important, but it was a mystery. They thought air was a gift from the gods. Only a god could breathe the breath of life into a living creature.

The wise men of many countries tried to find out the answers to these questions: What is air made of? Where does it come from? Why do people need air?

Earth, Air, Fire, and Water

The ancient Greeks tried to figure out how air gets into the body. One of them, Anaximenes, lived over 2,500 years ago. He believed that everything was made of air. He called it "pneuma," which means breath in Greek. Anaximenes believed that everything on the earth was alive and breathing. About a hundred years later, a man named Empedocles taught that everything was made out of four basic things, or **elements**. These elements were earth, air, fire, and water.

Empedocles studied the human body. He saw that **blood** travels around our bodies through tubes or **blood vessels**. He saw that the **heart** is at the center of the system of blood vessels. He said that blood vessels give a sort of heat to the body. This heat keeps us alive. Later, a very important Greek thinker named Aristotle agreed with him.

Aristotle said that the heart was like a fire. Breathing in air cooled the fire and kept it from burning up the whole body. About 1,700 years ago, the Roman Emperor's doctor was a man named Galen. He taught that the secret of life was a spirit, or "pneuma," that came from the air. This and other spirits flowed through the body and mixed with the blood. People believed Galen's ideas for the next 1,500 years.

▼ Aristotle taught that a special kind of heat inside the body keeps us alive. He believed that this heat came from the heart. The air we breathe was thought to keep the fire burning or cool the body down.

Finding Out

About 400 years ago, people began to take a new interest in science. New discoveries were made. In Italy around 1640, Evangelista Toricelli showed that air presses on things and makes them move. That is what we call **air pressure**. People used his ideas to make air pumps. Then, about twenty years later, an Englishman named Robert Hooke found out that parts of our bodies act like pumps. We use our chest, and the bones around it, our **ribs**, to pump air in and out of our lungs.

Air, Blood, and the Human Body

Other scientists had also begun to study how the body works. William Harvey was a very famous English doctor of the time. He showed that the heart pumps blood around the body. It sends the blood in one direction through large blood vessels. We call these **arteries**. The arteries carry blood to all parts of the body. Other blood vessels called **veins** carry the blood back to the heart.

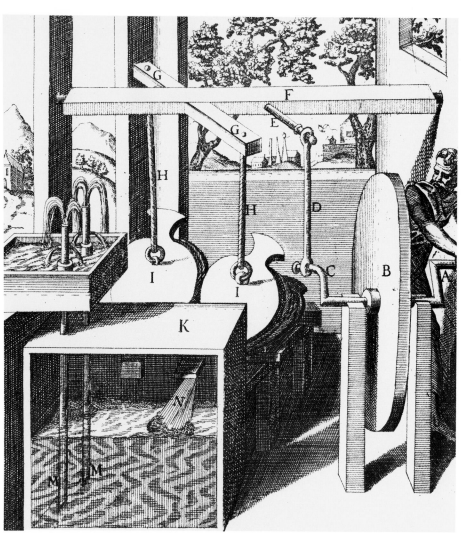

◀ In the 1600s, people learned how to make many new machines. This air pump was used to raise water through pipes. An understanding of machinery such as this helped scientists to discover how the human body works.

In 1609, an instrument called a **microscope** was invented in Holland. It was a great help to scientists because it made small things look larger. Robert Hooke described it in a book.

Later in that century, the microscope was used to look at the material of which our bodies are made up, called the **tissues**. It was found that the tissues of the body contain very tiny blood vessels, called **capillaries**. There are large numbers of capillaries in the walls of the lungs.

Then a man named John Mayow pointed out that air helps fires to burn. He thought that the air we breathe might help to burn certain substances in the body. He thought it might happen in the lung capillaries.

About a hundred years later, a French scientist named Antoine Lavoisier said that air is made up of two gases. He named them oxygen and **nitrogen**. His work showed that John Mayow was right. More recently, a German scientist, Otto Warburg, has shown how the body tissues use oxygen to help burn food for energy.

▶ Antoine Lavoisier was the first person to discover that air contains life-giving oxygen.

▼ This picture by Joseph Wright was painted in 1768. It shows a scientist trying out an air pump. Without air, the bird soon died. What was it in the air that kept the bird alive?

What Is Air?

The air around the earth is called the **atmosphere**. Oxygen is only one part of the atmosphere. The rest is a mixture of nitrogen, **carbon dioxide**, and several other gases such as **water vapor**. Along with these gases, there are always bits of dust in the atmosphere, too.

If you look at the diagram at the bottom of the page, you will see that the air you breathe out contains the same gases as the air you breathe in. However, the air you breathe out has less oxygen in it, and more carbon dioxide. Your body has used up most of the oxygen and replaced it with carbon dioxide.

Plants and Air

All animals use oxygen and make carbon dioxide as waste. They are doing this all the time. If nothing else happened, there would soon be no oxygen left. However, the amounts of oxygen and carbon dioxide in the atmosphere hardly change at all. This is because green plants use up carbon dioxide to make food. Plants take carbon dioxide from the air, and give back oxygen. This keeps the amount of oxygen in the air steady.

Air and Health

The air we breathe is not always clean. Often, it contains harmful materials. Even if we cannot see or smell them, they may be there. Our cars and factories and power plants all add these harmful **chemicals** to the atmosphere. When the chemicals in the air are mixed with smoke and dust, they may produce the kind of thick, dirty fog we call **smog**.

▼ Air is made up mostly of nitrogen, which the body cannot make use of. Air also contains oxygen, carbon dioxide, and other gases. The air you breathe out contains *less* oxygen and *more* carbon dioxide than the air you breathe in. This shows that your body uses up oxygen and makes carbon dioxide.

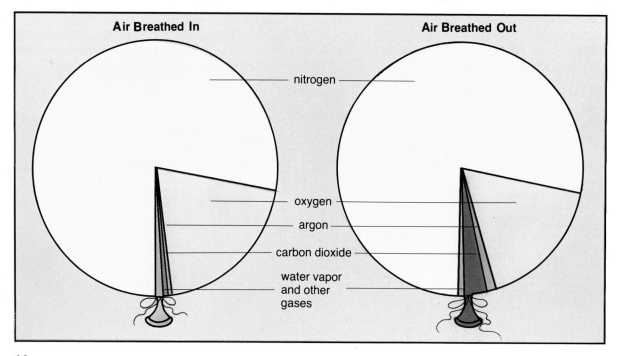

Air Breathed In — Air Breathed Out

nitrogen
oxygen
argon
carbon dioxide
water vapor and other gases

▲ Green plants take in the carbon dioxide that we breathe out. They make fresh oxygen which we breathe in. Too much carbon dioxide would poison us.

▶ Thick smog hangs over the city of Los Angeles. Foggy weather and the fumes from cars can make it difficult for people to breathe.

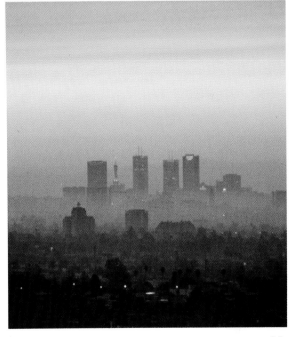

The word for what we do to spoil our air is **pollution**. Even when we spray our gardens to kill insects, we are adding to the pollution. Smog, or any kind of polluted air, can harm our lungs.

There are other harmful things in the air. These are the tiny living things that cause sickness and disease. They are known as **germs**. If we breathe them in, they may make us sick. However, our bodies have ways of destroying germs.

Why We Breathe

All living bodies must take in a constant supply of fresh air. Without the oxygen in fresh air anything alive soon dies. During breathing the body also makes waste which it must get rid of. The waste is in the form of carbon dioxide. The process of taking in oxygen and getting rid of carbon dioxide is called **respiration**.

The organs that the body uses to breathe make up the **respiratory system**. The most important of these organs are the two lungs inside the chest.

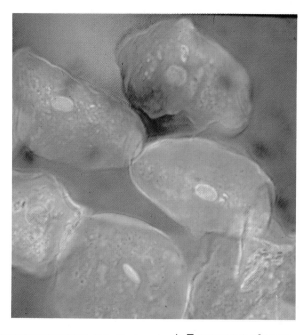

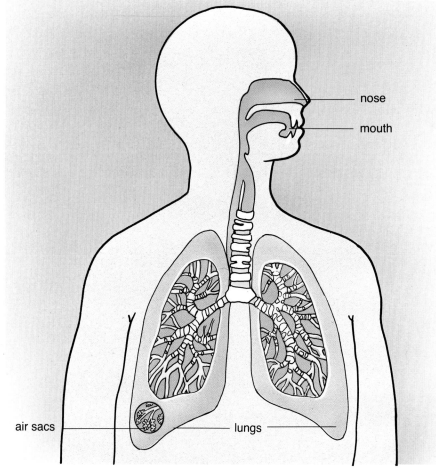

▲ Every part of your body is made up of tiny cells like these. You can only see them through a microscope. Everything that happens to make you live and grow happens inside these cells. Every cell in your body needs a supply of oxygen.

◀ Air gets into the body through the nose and mouth. You can see how air passes down tubes into your chest. The two lungs are in the center of your chest.

nose

mouth

air sacs — lungs —

Keeping the Body Alive

The human body, like all living things, is made up of millions of tiny units called **cells**. Each cell has its own job to do. A cell needs the strength, or **energy**, to do its job. Cells get this energy from the chemicals in food. The chemicals in the food and the oxygen in the blood get mixed together. They are changed into energy, carbon dioxide, and water.

Without oxygen, a cell may become damaged and die. Some cells can be damaged very easily by a lack of oxygen, so every cell must have a good supply. At the same time, the blood must get rid of the extra carbon dioxide which the body has made. Too much carbon dioxide in the blood is like a poison.

Around the Body

Respiration starts when we take in air through the nose and mouth. The air travels down a series of passages to the lungs. Once, people thought that there was an air passage from the lungs to the heart. Now, we know that the lungs put oxygen from the air into the blood vessels. The blood vessels take the oxygen to the heart. The heart then pumps it around the body.

In the end, the oxygen in the blood reaches the capillaries. The capillaries supply the body tissues with blood. Here the oxygen leaves the blood. Waste carbon dioxide takes its place. The carbon dioxide travels back to the lungs in the blood. The carbon dioxide is breathed out. More air is taken back into the lungs.

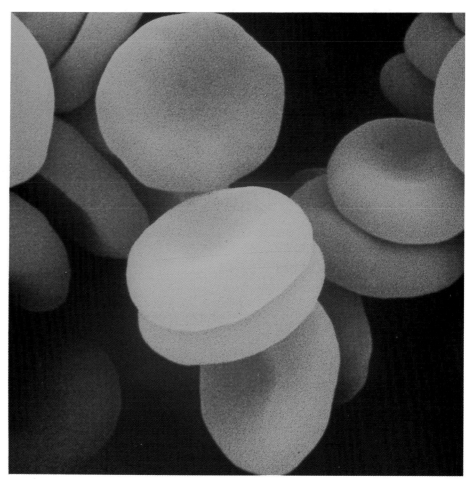

▶ Some cells in the blood take in oxygen from the lungs. The cells are round and flat. They are red. The cells carry oxygen from the lungs to the heart, which pumps the blood around the whole body.

Taking in Air

If you breathe in germs through your nose or mouth, you may catch a cold. Where do you feel it first? Is there a tickle in your nose? Does your nose run? Does your mouth feel dry? Do your ears ache? Is your throat sore? If you look at the diagram, you will see why. All these parts of the respiratory system open into one another. Therefore, when one part becomes infected, the other parts generally do, too.

▼ Little hairs inside your nose pick up dust and germs. The mucus in your nose collects the dust and germs. You blow your nose to get rid of the mucus. This helps you to breathe more easily.

▼ You breathe air in through your nose or mouth. Your nose, mouth, and air passages are all linked together.

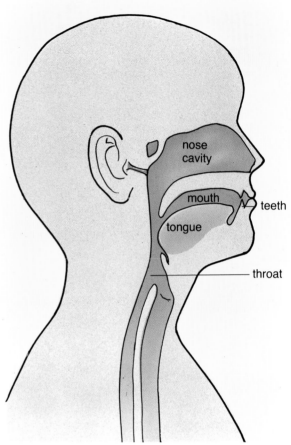

Inside Your Nose

Your nose makes the air warm, clean, and moist before it goes to the lungs. You take air into your nose through two openings called **nostrils**. Small hairs just inside the nostrils act like a strainer. They stop any dust or grit in the air from traveling into the space higher up in the nose, or the nose **cavity**. The nose cavity is divided in half by a thin wall of bone. It is lined with a moist tissue known as the **mucus membrane**. The mucus membrane produces the sticky **mucus** that you see when you blow your nose. Mucus produces water vapor and helps to remove dust from the air.

Cells at the top of the nose cavity give us our sense of smell. On each side of the cavity are three flat bones that stick out into the cavity. These bones help to warm up cold air or cool down hot air. They also help to make sure that any dust becomes trapped in mucus.

There are hollow spaces in the bones around the nose cavity. These are **sinuses**, and they help to make the bones in your head lighter.

Breathing through the Mouth

Air that you breathe through your mouth is not warmed. It is colder and drier than the air that you breathe through your nose. It is also dustier, because there is nothing in the mouth to remove the dust.

Air passes from the nose and mouth to a large tube in the throat called the **pharynx**. At the top of the pharynx are two lumps of tissue. These are the **tonsils**. They produce **white blood cells** that help destroy germs.

▶ There are cells high up in your nose which can detect smells. There are about fifteen different kinds of these cells. They help us to recognize more than 10,000 different smells! Our sense of smell also helps us to taste things.

Air and Speech

The pharynx is formed by the walls of **muscle** at the back of the nose, mouth, and throat. The air you breathe and the food you swallow all go down the pharynx. It leads to two tubes. One of these, the windpipe, or **trachea**, carries air to the lungs. The other, the **esophagus**, carries food to the stomach. The part of the body used for making speech called the **larynx**, is at the top of the trachea. Inside the larynx are two bands of tissue called the **vocal cords**.

It does not matter if air gets into your esophagus. If food gets into your trachea, however, you will start to choke. It does not happen often because there is a kind of trap door which closes the top of the trachea when you swallow. It is called the **epiglottis**. You cannot breathe through your mouth while you are swallowing. You cannot speak either. The vocal cords also close when you swallow.

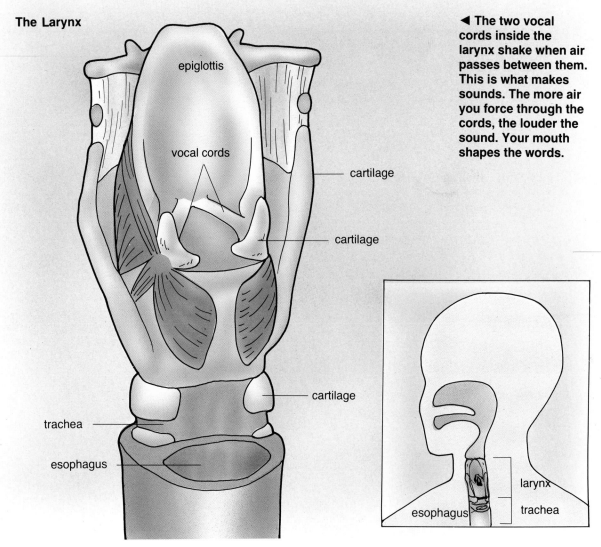

The Larynx

epiglottis

vocal cords

cartilage

cartilage

cartilage

trachea

esophagus

◀ The two vocal cords inside the larynx shake when air passes between them. This is what makes sounds. The more air you force through the cords, the louder the sound. Your mouth shapes the words.

larynx

trachea

esophagus

Making Sounds

Your larynx is made up of three pieces of a strong, elastic tissue known as **cartilage**. The front cartilage forms the lump in your throat which is often called the Adam's apple. The vocal cords are attached to the inside of the Adam's apple. They are also attached to two pieces of cartilage at the back of the larynx. When you speak or sing, air from your lungs passes through a small slit between the vocal cords. This makes the vocal cords vibrate rapidly, and they make a sound as the air goes through them.

To make different sounds you make your vocal cords looser or tighter. More or less air can pass through the slit. You shape the sounds into words by the movements of your lips and tongue.

▲ A singer makes sounds with the vocal cords in his larynx. The air you breathe goes down the trachea into your lungs. The voice box, or larynx, is at the top of this pipe. If you touch your throat when you are singing or speaking, you can feel where it is.

▼ A baby takes its first breath when it gives its first cry. Babies cannot ask for the things they need, so they cry. A baby tries out all sorts of sounds during its first year or two. First of all, it blows air through its lips or teeth. Then, it begins to make real words by using its lips and tongue.

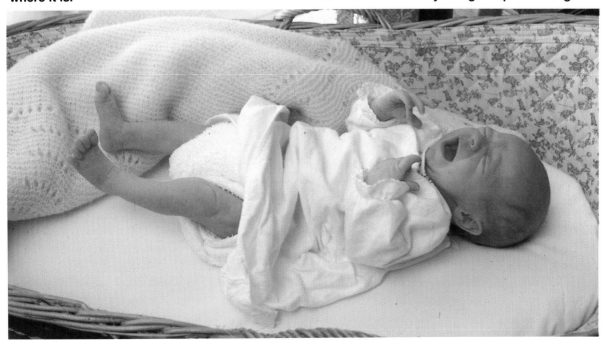

Into the Lungs

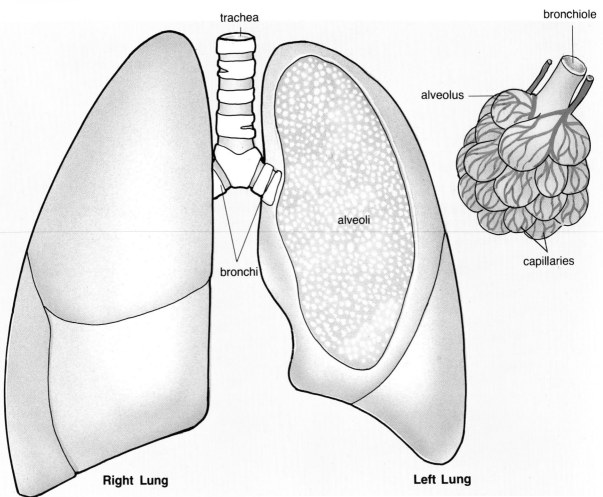

▼ In this picture you can see the outside of the right lung. You can look inside the left lung to see the millions of alveoli. They form a spongey mass. Air enters the alveoli through the bronchioles.

trachea

bronchiole

alveolus

alveoli

bronchi

capillaries

Right Lung

Left Lung

The trachea is about five inches long and about an inch wide. At its lower end, it divides into two smaller tubes known as the **bronchi**. Rings of tough cartilage make the trachea and the bronchi strong and help to keep them open.

Inside the lungs, the bronchi divide again and again into even smaller tubes called **bronchioles**. Each of these bronchioles end in something similar to a bunch of tiny balloons. Each balloon is an air sac. There are about 750 million of these tiny air sacs, or **alveoli**. If they were spread out and laid flat, they would cover a tennis court!

The trachea, the bronchi, and the larger bronchioles are lined with mucus membrane. This membrane produces mucus, which collects dust. The cells of the mucus membrane also have tiny hairs, called **cilia**, which sweep back and forth. This sweeping action of the cilia moves the mucus and the dust back towards the mouth.

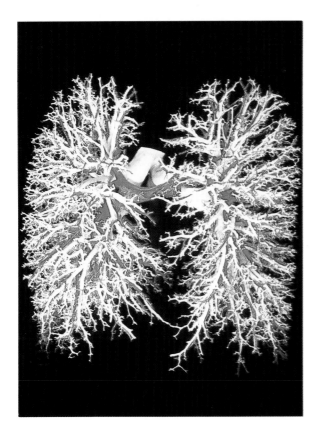

The Lungs

The lungs lie in a space in the chest called the chest cavity. They look like greyish pink bags. Deep cracks divide the right lung into three parts. The left lung is divided into two parts. Each lung is covered by two smooth, shining membranes. These are called the **pleural membranes**. The outer membrane is attached to the inside of the chest cavity. The inner one makes a kind of pocket for the lung. The pleural membranes are moist and slippery, so that the lungs do not rub against the ribs.

Inside the lungs, the bronchioles branch out into more and more tubes. There are several bunches of alveoli at the tip of each tiny bronchiole. Each alveolus has its own supply of blood. A small artery divides into capillaries. These surround each alveolus. Blood in the capillaries draws oxygen from the air in the alveoli. Then, the blood is collected by a small vein.

▲ In this model of the inside of a lung, air passages are shown in white and blood vessels in red.

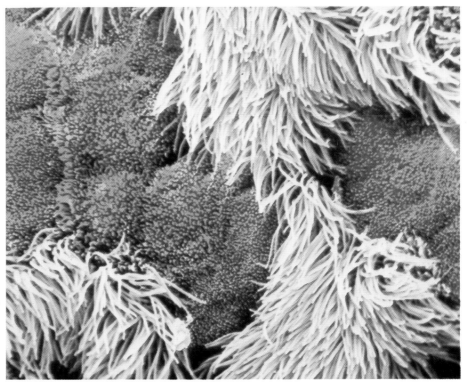

► When they are seen through a microscope, cilia in the lung look like grass blown by the wind. The cilia protect the lungs from dust.

Into the Blood

Each alveolus and each capillary is lined with a single layer of cells. The oxygen mixes with the moisture on the wall of the alveolus and becomes liquid or fluid. Then, it mixes with the fluid of the two layers of cells. Next, it flows into the blood itself. In the blood, the oxygen is drawn into the **red blood cells**. These cells get their color from a bright red coloring called **hemoglobin**.

▼ Inside each alveolus, one gas is exchanged for another. Oxygen in the air that has been breathed in passes into the blood. It is replaced by carbon dioxide from the blood that the body has used. The air is then breathed out.

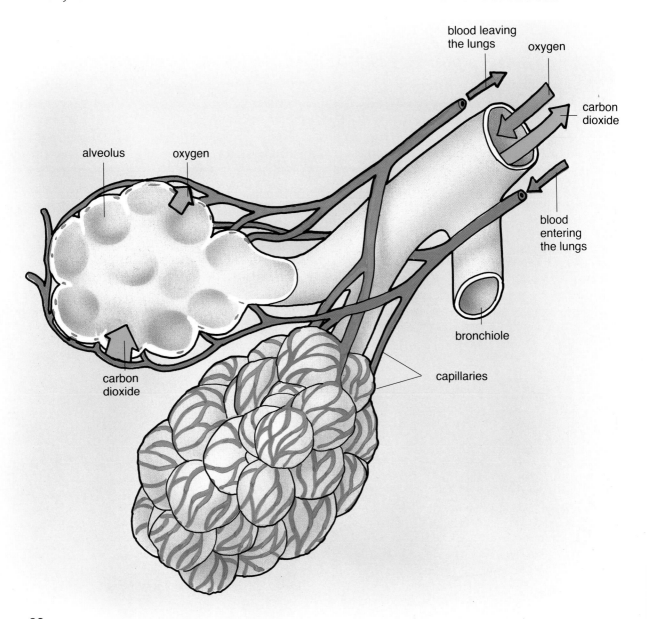

blood leaving the lungs

oxygen

carbon dioxide

blood entering the lungs

alveolus

oxygen

bronchiole

carbon dioxide

capillaries

▶ The left hand side of your heart pumps blood from the lungs to all parts of the body. The right hand side of your heart pumps blood back into the lungs.

▼ The blood is pumped from the heart to the body tissues through the arteries. It returns to the heart through the veins. Here, blood that is rich in oxygen is shown in red. Blood that is richer in carbon dioxide is shown in blue.

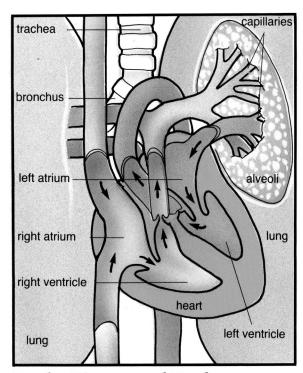

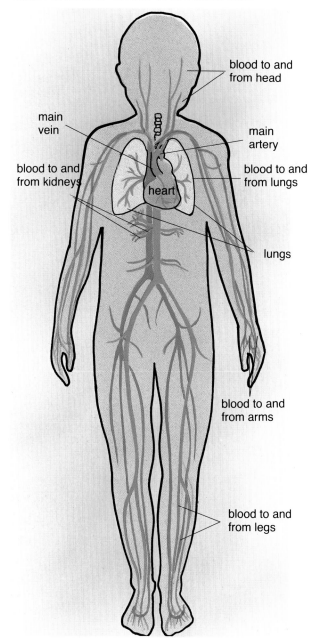

To the Tissues and Back

Oxygen combines with the hemoglobin in the blood. When the blood leaves the lungs, it is bright red and rich in oxygen. Large veins carry the blood to the heart.

The heart is divided into four parts. The upper part on the left side of the heart receives the blood from the lungs. This is the left **atrium**. The lower part, the left **ventricle**, then pumps the blood along the main arteries to the smaller arteries, and then to the tiny capillaries in the body tissues. Here the blood gives up its oxygen to the cells around the capillaries.

In order to take in the oxygen, the cells must first get rid of waste carbon dioxide. Like oxygen, carbon dioxide travels mostly in the red blood cells. It does not combine with hemoglobin however. It also travels in the clear fluid around the red blood cells. The blood now travels back through the veins to the right side of the heart. The right ventricle pumps the blood back to the lungs. The whole journey around the body takes less than a minute.

How the Lungs Work

Robert Hooke was the first person to notice that our ribs and chest muscles use the pressure of the air to draw air into our lungs.

The ribs form a cage around the chest cavity. At the bottom of the **rib cage** the cavity is sealed by a sheet of muscle. This sheet of muscle is called the **diaphragm**. When the diaphragm is relaxed, it curves upward into the chest cavity.

When you breathe in, the diaphragm tightens. It is drawn downward until it is flat. The rib muscles tighten and the ribs move upward and outward. The space inside the chest cavity gets larger. Now the pressure of the air inside the cavity is less than it was. To keep the air pressure the same inside and outside the lungs, the lungs suck in air.

When you breathe out, all the muscles relax. This makes the chest cavity smaller. Then, the lungs push air out. At least one and a half quarts of air stays in the lungs all the time. This keeps them from collapsing completely.

▼ In order to draw air into the lungs, the ribs lift and the chest cavity gets bigger. The lungs stretch. Then, when the breathing muscles relax, the lungs shrink. This forces the breath out.

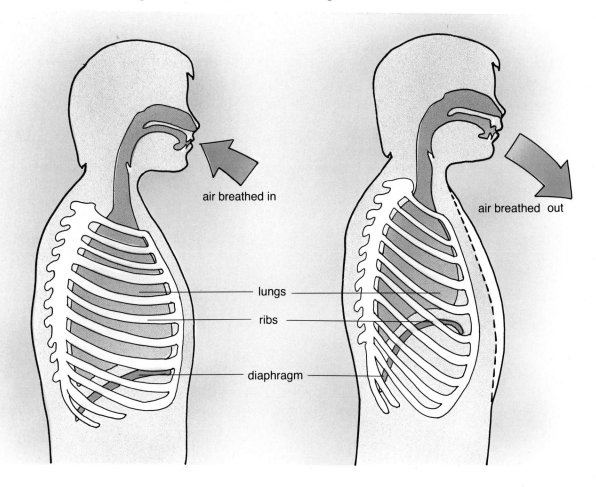

air breathed in

air breathed out

lungs

ribs

diaphragm

Breathing Control

When you are breathing quietly, you take between fifteen and twenty breaths each minute. An adult breathes about half a quart of air in and out with each breath.

However, when you get more exercise, you need more energy. Your muscles need more oxygen. You need to breathe more quickly and more deeply. An adult may take in four quarts of air in a deep breath.

Normally, you breathe without thinking. Your breathing is controlled by a part of your brain called the **respiratory center**. When the amount of carbon dioxide in your blood increases, this center sends out signals to make you breathe faster.

◄ When you play games like basketball, your body muscles need extra oxygen. They get it when you breathe faster and deeper than normal. Your heart speeds up to pump blood quickly around your body.

▶ Our lungs hold about the same amount of air as a party balloon, but you cannot blow up a balloon in one breath. This is because some air always stays in the lungs.

Hiccups and Sneezes

▼ A yawn may be a sign of boredom or tiredness. It also seems to be catching! If you see someone yawn, you often start to yawn yourself. Even talking or thinking about yawning may make you want to yawn.

Breathing is not always easy or quiet. Sometimes, it is hard to breathe. Sometimes, it hurts. Sometimes, it makes a noise. The noise it makes may be a cough, a sneeze, or a hiccup.

Why Do We Hiccup?

A hiccup happens when your diaphragm suddenly tightens. This is called a **spasm**. Then, air rushes into the lungs. At the same time, the upper opening of the larynx, called the **glottis**, snaps shut. This produces the sound of the hiccup.

You may get hiccups if you eat too quickly or if you are excited. Sometimes, they are a problem. One man in the United States has been hiccuping ever since 1922! You may be able to stop the hiccups by holding your breath. Usually, they stop when you think about something else.

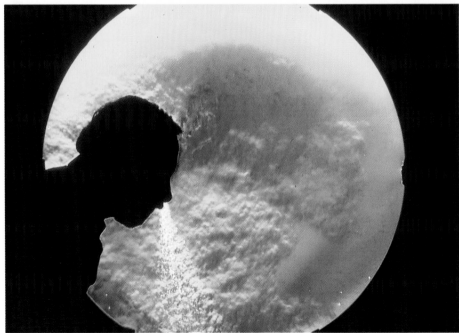

◄ Sneezing is the natural thing to do if something is tickling your nose. Unfortunately, sneezes spread germs. This photograph shows the particles produced by a sneeze.

Why Do We Yawn?

We do not usually yawn on purpose. A yawn just happens. The air is slowly sucked in and then released. We seem to yawn most when we are tired or if the room is very stuffy. A yawn may be the body's way of getting more oxygen, in order to feel more alert.

Coughs and Sneezes

We cannot help coughing and sneezing. We do it if there is something in the air passages that is tickling them or blocking them. We sneeze or cough in order to get rid of the irritating material as fast as we can.

To make a cough, the lungs are loaded somewhat like an air rifle. The glottis is closed. Then, the muscles of the stomach squeeze the air in the chest. The glottis is forced to open, and the air rushes out at high speed.

You sneeze when something tickles the membrane that lines the inside of your nose. Your tongue rises to close the back of the mouth and a blast of air from the lungs is forced out through the nose. The blast of air may reach a speed of a hundred miles per hour! Some people cannot stop sneezing. One British girl sneezed about 20 times a day for 977 days.

Coughs and sneezes spread germs. When you cough or sneeze, you can spray a lot of mucus a very long way through the air. This mucus may carry germs. Germs, as you know, can make people sick.

▼ The air you breathe out contains a lot of water vapor. On a cold day, the vapor turns into drops of water. Your breath is hotter than the air around you, so what you see is steam.

Checking the Lungs

Doctors use instruments to make sure that your lungs are healthy. They can listen to sounds in your chest with a **stethoscope**. They can also take pictures of your lungs and other organs inside your body.

Listening to the Chest

The stethoscope was invented in 1815 by a French doctor named René Laënnec. He used a long wooden tube to listen to the noises in his patients' chests. A modern stethoscope has rubber tubes that lead from a piece shaped like a cup to two ear pieces. When a doctor listens to your lungs, he or she is listening to the sounds the air makes as you breathe in and out. It should be a soft, rustling sound. However, if germs have attacked the lungs or

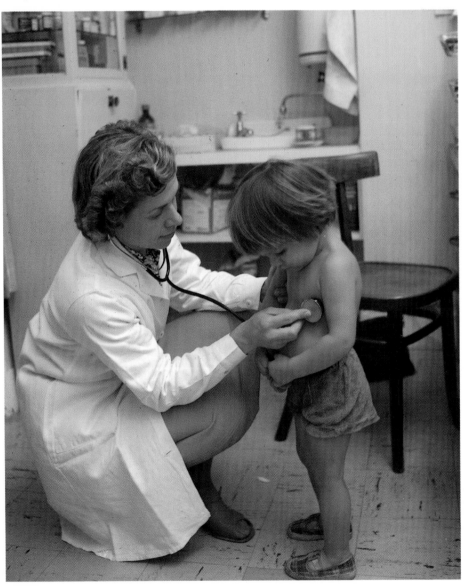

◄ This doctor is listening to the air as it moves in and out of the child's lungs. Doctors know how to tell if there is anything wrong with your lungs by the sounds your breathing makes.

▶ Until about 100 years ago, doctors could only guess what was wrong inside a patient's chest. Today, they can make a picture of your lungs. You lie still in under the X-ray machine. The machine makes a buzzing noise and the rays pass through the body. You do not feel anything.

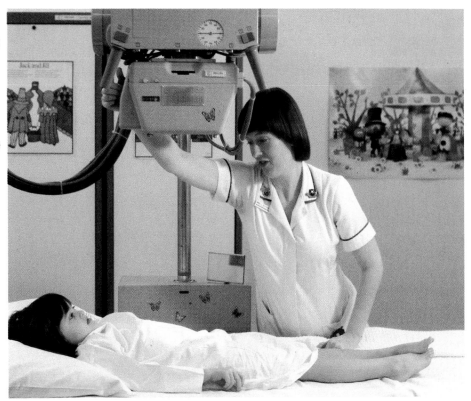

bronchi, the doctor may hear squeaking, creaking, or whistling noises. These could be a sign that the germs have caused an **infection** in the lungs.

Looking Inside

Doctors use **X-rays** to examine the inside of your body. You cannot see or feel X-rays, even though they pass through skin and muscle. However, the organs inside your body where the X-rays stop show up on the X-ray pictures. Some organs show up better than others. You can also see your bones very clearly. X-ray pictures help doctors to see what is happening inside any part of the body.

Doctors use chest X-rays to look at people's lungs. In this way, they can find out whether people's lungs show any signs of disease.

Too many X-rays can harm your body. Doctors only take an X-ray of your chest if there are signs of infection.

▼ A chest X-ray is held up to the light. The doctor can see the patient's lungs, ribs, and backbone. The doctor can tell at once if there is any trace of a disease in the lungs.

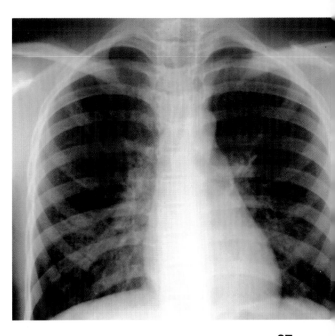

Breathing Problems

The membrane that lines the air passages and lungs is very delicate. The lungs have to take in air from the world outside, but that air may be polluted. Any dust or germs in the air may harm the membrane.

The disease that most often attacks the air passages is the common cold. Cold germs make the membrane swollen and make it feel sore. The membrane is **inflamed**. It produces mucus to help prevent the germs from spreading. You start to sneeze. The germs attack the lining of the nose, but they may reach the sinuses, the throat, and the larynx.

◄ During the spring and summer, flowering plants make pollen. This is blown about by the wind. Pollen in the air makes it hard for some people to breathe. They get watery eyes and a runny nose.

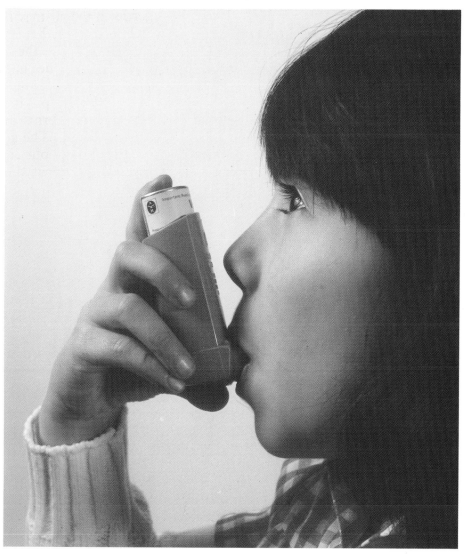

► This child has asthma, and is using a spray to help her breathe. The spray contains a drug that relaxes the muscles of the bronchioles. This allows air to flow into the lungs more easily.

Your body, however, is fighting the infection. The cold usually gets better in a few days. Doctors have not yet found a way to stop or cure the common cold.

Other Problems

Sometimes, the trouble is more serious. Germs can infect the bronchi, sinuses, larynx, pharynx, and tonsils, and make people very sick. Often, children suffer from infections of the tonsils. **Bronchitis** is a common disease caused by germs which infect the bronchi and make them inflamed.

In the early summer, grasses and other plants make large amounts of a yellow dust called **pollen**. Breathing in pollen bothers many people. The lining of their air passages reacts to the pollen by becoming inflamed. They get **hay fever**. A reaction like this to something we eat or touch or breathe is called an **allergy**.

An allergy to pollen, house dust, and other things is often the cause of **asthma**. If the tubes to the lungs become inflamed and swollen, the muscles around them may go into a spasm. The tubes tighten, and it is hard for the patient to breathe.

Fighting Diseases

▼ Louis Pasteur was a French scientist. He was the first person to prove that germs cause diseases. Pasteur found a way of heating wine to kill the germs in it. We still use the same method to kill the germs in milk. This has helped to prevent the spread of tuberculosis.

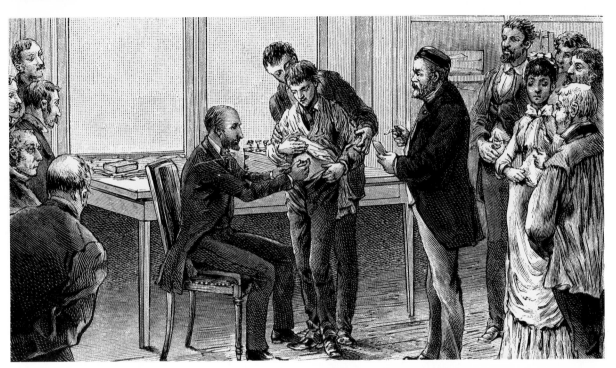

Many diseases affect our lungs. Germs may cause the lungs to become very inflamed, and this can cause **pneumonia**. The patient gets a fever, a cough, and pain in the chest. An infection of the pleural membranes around the lungs is called **pleurisy**. The membranes become inflamed and rub against each other. This is very painful. One kind of germ when breathed into the lungs causes small lumps to form. This disease is called **tuberculosis**. The patient coughs, has a fever, and may cough up blood. After a time, parts of the lung may be destroyed.

▶ This man is spraying the plants with chemicals which will kill harmful insects. If he breathed in the chemicals, they would harm his lungs. Therefore, he wears a mask over his nose and mouth.

The most serious disease of the lungs is **cancer**. The lung tissue grows out of shape and forms a lump. The cells with cancer divide and spread. They destroy other healthy cells. Smoking cigarettes is one cause of lung cancer.

Some lung diseases are caused by the work people do. Coal dust damages the lungs of coal miners. Dust from broken rocks can harm the lungs of the people who dig it up or work with it. Some building materials, like asbestos, are no longer used. We know now that they are harmful to the lungs.

Healthy Lungs

Tuberculosis used to kill many people. It still does in places where people live close together and in bad housing. Tuberculosis is not so common now. People can be given a very weak dose of the germ. The germ is not strong enough to harm the people. Their bodies learn to fight the disease. We call this a **vaccination**. Cows' milk once carried tuberculosis. Now the milk can be heated to kill any germs which are in it. There are also new drugs which help to cure anyone who catches the disease.

Most other lung diseases can also be stopped or cured. People know that it is important to keep their homes warm and dry and to breathe clean air. We have laws that help to reduce air pollution. We have laws to guard the health and safety of people at work in factories and in coal mines. We have drugs with which to treat infections in our lungs.

We still need to find a way to stop cancer. A great deal of time and money is being spent on this. For a start, the governments in many countries are telling people to stop smoking.

▼ This boy is being tested to see if he has had tuberculosis. If he has not, he will be vaccinated so that he does not get it.

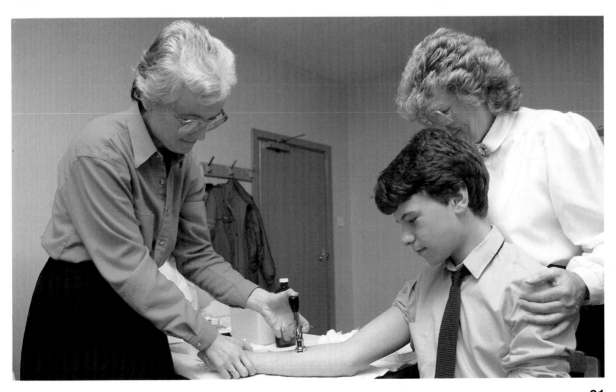

Modern Treatments

Fifty years ago, anyone with a serious lung disease was expected to die. Today, using modern machines, doctors can keep their patients alive even if their lungs are not working at all.

A machine called a **ventilator** pumps air into a patient's lungs through a tube that goes into the windpipe. A computer controls the amounts of oxygen and carbon dioxide in the blood.

If the lungs need a rest, doctors have a machine to take their place. It is called an **artificial lung**. A tube takes blood from a main vein in the leg to the artificial lung. Then, the machine adds oxygen to the blood and pipes it back into the main artery of the leg.

▲ How strongly can you blow? This instrument measures puffing power. It helps doctors to tell if the lungs are working properly.

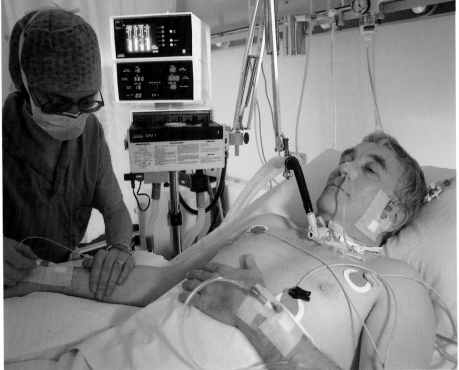

◄ If a patient's lungs are not working well, a ventilator may be used to do the job. This machine takes warm, moist air to the patient's lungs. It checks the amount and the pressure of the air that goes in. It checks the mixture of gases in the air that the patient breathes out. If anything goes wrong, an alarm rings.

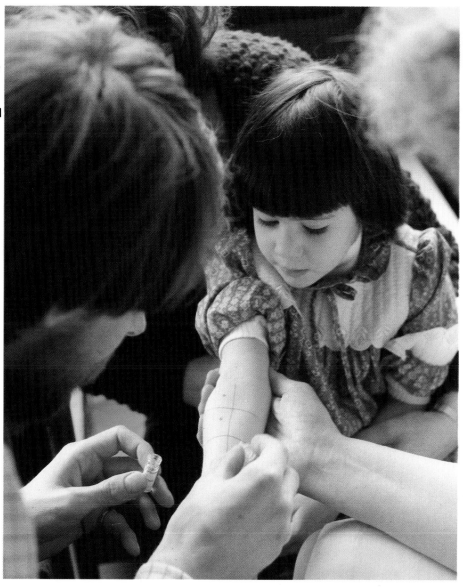

► Doctors have become very skilful at finding out about allergies. For example, asthma may be caused by animal hairs or pollen. Here a child is being tested to see if she is allergic to various substances.

Doctors can also take healthy lungs from someone who has died. Doctors who do this are called **surgeons**. The person with the healthy lungs will have died from some other disease or in an accident. The surgeons can put the healthy lungs into someone who has bad lungs. This is called **transplant** surgery.

What the Surgeon Can Do

When a surgeon cuts into a patient's body, we call it an operation.

Lung diseases are not easy to treat with surgery. Lung cancer can sometimes be cured by an operation in the early stages. Surgeons have even transplanted a heart and lungs together. It was possible to do this because the heart and lungs are so closely connected to each other in the body. Surgeons can also place a tube in a patient's trachea by cutting a hole in the outer wall of the throat. They do this if something is blocking the larynx. If the larynx is diseased, surgeons can remove it.

Operations

When surgeons carry out an operation, they use a sharp knife, called a scalpel, to cut through skin and muscle. They also have to cut through the telephone lines of the body, that is, the **nerves**. The nerves carry signals to the brain. If a nerve is cut, the patient feels pain.

Surgeons do not want their patients to suffer, so they give them drugs to block pain. These drugs are called **anesthetics**. Anesthetics put the nerves to sleep. The nerves do not send signals to the brain, so the patient does not feel pain. Some of the anesthetics put the patient completely to sleep. They make the patient **unconscious**.

A Mixture of Gases

In the past, doctors tried many different drugs to reduce the pain of operations. They collected drugs from plants like the opium poppy, henbane, and mandrake.

▼ The first surgeons to use real anesthetics chose ether, chloroform, or laughing gas. Breathing in gases made the patient sleepy.

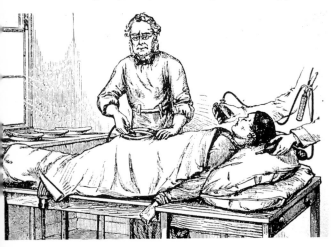

They tried using alcohol to relax the patient. Many operations were carried out without using any drugs at all. The surgeon had to work quickly! Even then, patients often died from shock.

The first anesthetics that really worked were discovered during the 1840's. An American doctor used a gas called **ether** to make a patient unconscious while he removed a lump from the patient's neck. The patient breathed in the ether through his nose and mouth. A year later, a London doctor used a gas called **chloroform** in the same way.

People have known for a very long time that plants like mandrake make people relaxed and sleepy. However, these medicines could not stop people feeling pain, as modern anesthetics can.

A Deep Sleep

Today, the person who gives a patient an anesthetic is called the **anesthetist**. It is a difficult job. Anesthetists use a wide range of drugs and gases. Patients are given a drug to make them feel sleepy. The anesthetist also uses drugs to control the way the body works. Some drugs keep the mouth dry. Others relax the muscles.

When the patient is very relaxed he may not breathe very deeply. He is given extra oxygen to make sure that there is plenty of this vital gas in the blood.

Patients may react badly to some drugs. If too many drugs are given, the patient may stop breathing! The anesthetist has to watch closely to make sure that nothing goes wrong during an operation.

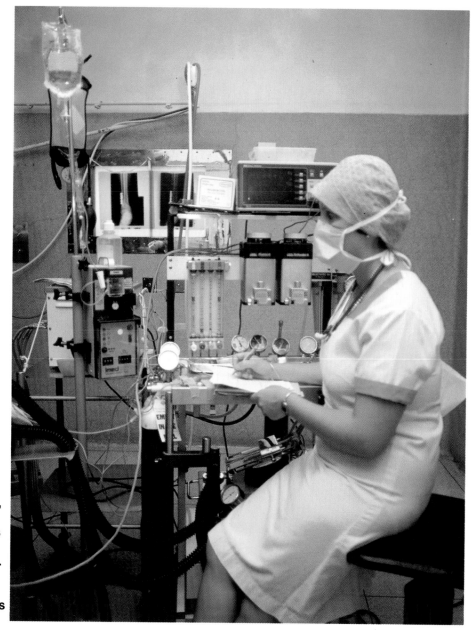

▶ At each operation, the anesthetist decides which drugs to give the patient and in what quantity. She makes sure that the patient stays asleep and continues breathing.

To the Rescue

If someone near you is gasping for air or starts to choke, what can you do? First of all, do not panic. If you are going to be of any use, you must stay calm and think clearly. Then you may be able to help by giving first aid.

Aid means help. First aid is the help a person gets until the doctor or the paramedics arrive. Perhaps a friend has nearly drowned. If you know what to do, you could save his or her life.

You may learn about first aid at school. You can read about it in books. Some schools or youth clubs offer first aid classes. These classes give you a chance to practice first aid yourself.

During an emergency, if you are not sure what to do, call an adult quickly. Telephone for an ambulance. Do you know the emergency numbers in your area? Find out what they are. Then write them down and keep them near the telephone.

Things You Can Do

If someone has trouble breathing, there are simple things anyone can do. You may know why your friend is having a bad attack of asthma. Lead him or her away from the dusty area or the hairy dog. Take him or her indoors, where there is less pollen in the air. Help him or her to relax and keep calm.

People gasping for breath can breathe more easily if you loosen their collars, ties or belts.

If people stop breathing, they must be made to start again quickly. Trained people do this by giving mouth-to-mouth resuscitation. Do not try it yourself unless you have been trained by a certified instructor.

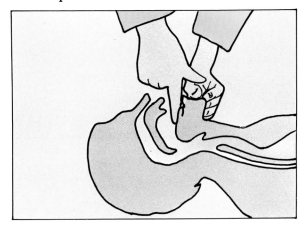

▲ Trained first-aiders know how to give mouth-to-mouth resuscitation to people who have stopped breathing. First, they make sure that the person's throat is not blocked by the tongue.

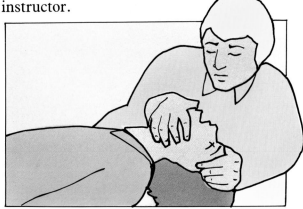

▲ The first-aider tips back the person's head. Nothing must stop air from getting into the nose or throat. The first-aider then holds the person's nose and breathes into the mouth, or else closes the person's mouth and blows air into their nose.

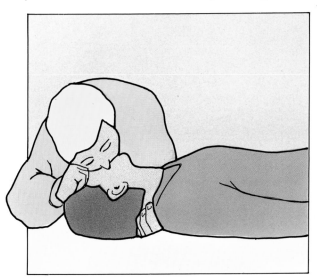

▲ The first four breaths are given quickly, to clear the air passages. The breathing should then be slowed to about sixteen to eighteen breaths per minute.

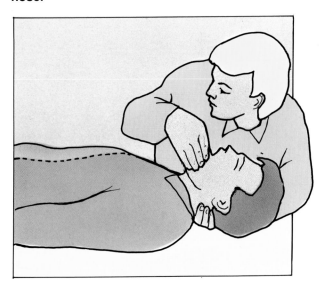

▲ Each of the first-aider's breaths fills the victim's lungs with air. Time must be allowed for the lungs to push out the air. The chest must be checked to see if it is rising and falling.

Keeping Healthy

Your body needs exercise. Like the parts of a machine, the parts of your body work best when they are used. When you walk or run or swim or play sports, you are improving the strength of your muscles. You can keep going longer without getting tired. Your muscles need oxygen to work, so exercise makes your heart and lungs work, too.

Lung Stretchers

Exercise can improve your ability to take in oxygen. Any kind of exercise that you do steadily for more than twenty minutes will increase your ability to breathe.

Distance running, swimming, bicycling, and walking are all good for your lungs.

Your muscles need a constant supply of oxygen when you exercise, so you need to breathe deeply and often. This makes your breathing muscles strong. It increases the amount of air you can take into your lungs. At the same time, your heart muscle works harder and faster too. You can feel the blood rush around your body. The extra activity strengthens the heart and lungs.

▼ Regular exercise is good for the lungs and the heart. It keeps them strong. A healthy body needs plenty of oxygen. Steady exercise over a lengthy period helps your body take in a lot of oxygen.

It is better to exercise three or four times a week for fifteen or twenty minutes than to do it all at once. Warm up with a slow start and cool off by slowing down before the end. It is better for your heart and lungs.

Short Bursts

Some forms of exercise, like sprinting and weight lifting, use a lot of energy in a very short time. Your muscles use oxygen faster than you can replace it. However, energy is then made by a process that uses no oxygen. This process makes a chemical which builds up in your muscles. Too much of this chemical will cause pain, so you cannot do this kind of exercise for very long.

When you stop exercising, you must breathe deeply. Then your lungs will send a fresh supply of oxygen to the muscles.

▲ Throwing the javelin requires strength and athletic skill. It makes use of a short burst of energy. This kind of exercise does not help the body take in oxygen.

► A bicycle ride is not only fun, but a good way to keep healthy. Fresh air supplies the oxygen which keeps our muscles working.

Breathing Deeply

The respiratory center in your brain makes sure that your breathing muscles work all the time. You do not have to think about it. You breathe even if you are unconscious. You breathe when you are asleep. However, you can change the way you breathe if you want to.

You can hold your breath. If you hold it for too long, you will feel dizzy and faint. Your brain will run out of oxygen. When you faint, you start to breathe again. Sometimes people who are very upset take many short, deep breaths in a row. This is called **hyperventilating**. Hyperventilating is bad because the carbon dioxide in the body decreases. Then the blood cannot exchange gases correctly.

▲ This woman will soon be having a baby. She is learning breathing exercises. These will help her during the birth.

◄ Singers must also be trained to breathe deeply. If they were to take a deep breath in the middle of their singing, they might ruin the music!

40

► Breathing control is a very important part of yoga. This man is being taught how to breathe deeply by his yoga teacher.

Take a Deep Breath

Breathing correctly is good for your health. You should learn to breathe in through your nose and out through your mouth. The nose filters out dust and germs before they reach the lungs.

Breathing deeply and slowly exercises your diaphragm and rib muscles. It helps the blood to get rid of waste matter. If you empty the lungs fully when you breathe out, you get rid of the carbon dioxide. More fresh oxygen will be able to get into your lungs.

Breathing deeply helps you to keep calm. Try taking a deep breath if you feel nervous or excited. It will help you if you want to pass a test, win a race, or act in a play. Some women learn deep breathing before their babies are born. It helps them to relax while they are giving birth.

Yoga is a system of exercise that helps to make people strong. Deep breathing is an important part of yoga. It strengthens the mind as well as the body. You can learn breathing exercises from books or by joining a yoga class.

Smoking and Health

Every year, over 300,000 people in the United States die as a result of smoking. A person who does not smoke is likely to live for fifteen or twenty years longer than a person who does smoke. You will be healthier all your life if you do not smoke.

Smoking Is Bad for You

It is the drug called nicotine in tobacco that makes people keep smoking. The nicotine is carried to the brain very quickly. The drug makes changes in the brain. People who smoke then want more nicotine or they do not feel good. Smoking a cigarette becomes a habit. It is a harmful habit, however. A poisonous gas has been found in tobacco smoke. Doctors think smoking may lead to heart attacks. Also, there is carbon dioxide in tobacco smoke which is not good for the body.

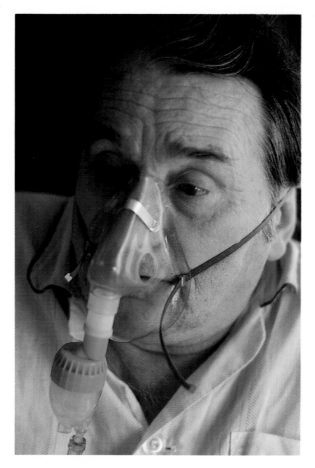

▲ This man is suffering from a disease caused by smoking cigarettes. He has to wear a special mask to help him breathe.

Tobacco smoke contains tar. If a smoker blows smoke through a handkerchief, the tar makes a dark brown stain. This is what smokers breathe into their lungs.

Tar spreads over the mucous membranes that line the air passages and lungs. The tar makes them sore. They become inflamed and swollen. This can lead to bronchitis.

◀ One mouthful of cigarette smoke blown through a handkerchief leaves behind a smear of brown tar. Think of the amount of tar left on the lungs by cigarettes, and of the harm it can do.

The tiny hair-like cilia that help to get rid of waste matter get covered with tar. They cannot do their job of keeping the lungs clean. Then, the inflamed membranes are attacked by germs. In many cases, this leads to cancer of the lungs, throat, or mouth.

The easy flow of oxygen and carbon dioxide in and out of the blood slows down. The smoker finds it hard to breathe.

No Smoking!

Smoking is not the only thing that is bad for our lungs. However, it is something that we can control. Smokers do harm to their lungs. They pollute the air.

At one time, people thought it was glamorous to smoke. Movie stars and other famous people smoked all the time. Now, people know about the harm tobacco can do. Many people who used to smoke have quit. Fewer people are beginning to smoke in the first place.

▼ No one likes to breathe in the smoke of other people's cigarettes, which is bad for our health. Smoking is banned in movie theaters and often in other public places, too. In some countries it is forbidden to advertise cigarettes on television. In the U.S., tobacco companies must print health warnings on each package of cigarettes.

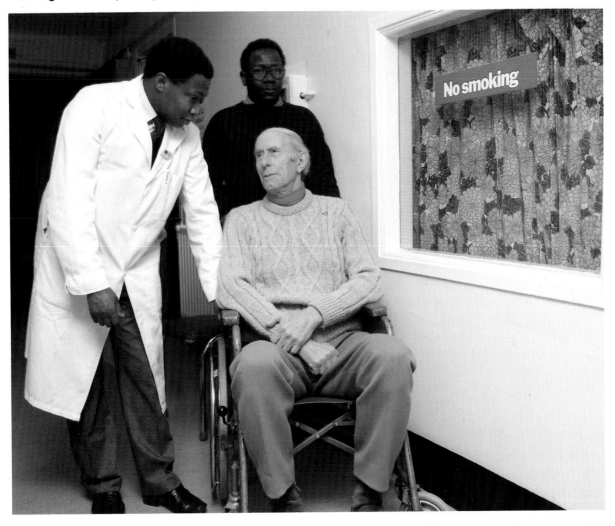

New Worlds

▼ A scuba diver explores a coral reef. He can breathe in air from the tanks on his back. Humans have learned to survive in many places where they cannot breathe naturally.

Human beings breathe air. Our lungs are made to keep us alive in the earth's atmosphere. We cannot live without air. We cannot breathe in space, where there is no atmosphere. We cannot breathe under water, either. We can visit both of these places, but we need to take a supply of air with us.

Taking Air with Us

Deep-sea divers used to have air pumped down to them from a ship. Modern divers carry bottles filled with air on their backs. When they breathe in, they get air through an air tube that runs from the air supply to their mouths. When they breathe out, the carbon dioxide is let out into the water, and makes a stream of bubbles. The air pressure changes as they dive deeper. The divers breathe in ordinary air when they first enter the water. However, when divers go more than 200 feet down, they must breathe a mixture of gases to keep bubbles of nitrogen from forming in the blood. If this happens, a diver will get **the bends**. The bends are very painful and can even cause death. A diver gets the bends if he comes up toward the surface too fast.

Divers who go very far beneath the surface use special diving suits or ships built for the purpose. They are able to withstand the great pressure.

Travelers in space also carry their own air supply. The air pressure inside a spaceship is the same as it is on the Earth. The air must be kept clean. The carbon dioxide that is breathed out is taken away. When people stay longer in space, they will use green plants to take in the carbon dioxide and to make oxygen.

Outside the spaceship, people must wear spacesuits. They breathe oxygen from a bottle on their backs. Oxygen at the correct pressure fills the whole suit.

In the Future

Our earth is getting crowded. Someday, we may want to live under the sea or out in space. People living in a space city might use plants and sunlight to make the oxygen they would need to live there. People living in underwater cities might build special machines to filter oxygen from the sea or use long tubes that would bring oxygen down from the surface.

▼ There is no air in space. Astronauts have to carry an air supply with them. Perhaps one day, we shall build vast spacecraft which will be like miniature worlds. They would be filled with air. People could live and breathe there, and grow plants.

Glossary

air pressure: the way in which the layers of air press down on the earth.

allergy: an illness caused when something such as dust has an unusual effect on the body. Hay fever is an allergy caused by pollen.

alveoli: tiny thin-walled sacs that are filled with air. They are found at the end of the smaller air passages of the lungs.

anesthetic: something that makes people or animals lose their sense of pain or feeling.

anesthetist: the person in a hospital who is responsible for making sure that a patient does not feel any pain during an operation.

artery: a tube which carries fresh blood away from the heart to all parts of the body.

artificial lung: a machine used to take air into and out of the blood when the lungs are not working.

asthma: an illness which makes it difficult to breathe properly. The breathing tubes in the body become swollen or close up completely.

atmosphere: the layer of gases which surrounds a planet or star. The earth's atmosphere is the air.

atrium: one of the two small chambers at the top of the heart.

bends, the: a painful illness when bubbles of nitrogen gas form in the blood because of a sudden change in the pressure of the air. Divers get the bends if they rise up from very deep water too quickly.

blood: a liquid found inside the body. It has a red color and carries food, oxygen, and other important things to every part of the body.

blood vessel: any tube which carries the blood around inside your body.

bronchi: the two breathing tubes which are joined to the lungs. Each bronchus takes air to and from one of the lungs.

bronchitis: a disease during which the bronchi become swollen and sore.

bronchioles: the very small breathing tubes that branch off the bronchi and carry air inside the lungs.

cancer: a very serious illness which sometimes attacks the lungs. Cancer will cause the material which makes up the lungs to grow out of shape and form a lump. The illness can then spread to other parts of the body.

capillary: a very tiny tube which carries blood in and out of every part of the body.

carbon dioxide: a gas made up of carbon and oxygen. We breathe it out as waste.

cartilage: a tough, rubbery material found in various parts of the body. It helps to hold your bones together.

cavity: a space inside something.

cell: a very small part or unit of a living animal or plant. Most living things are made up of millions of cells.

chemical: any substance which can change when joined or mixed with another substance.

chloroform: a colorless liquid with a strong, sweet smell. When you breathe it in it can put you to sleep.

cilia: tiny hairs which grow in parts of the body such as the nose and lungs. The cilia beat backward and forward to sweep dust and dirt out of the body.

diaphragm: a flat sheet of muscle that lies under your lungs. The diaphragm can get shorter or longer, and this makes your lungs work.

element: one of the many basic materials from which everything in the universe is made.

energy: the power to do work. People get energy from food. Engines get energy from fuel like gasoline.

epiglottis: a flap of tissue behind the tongue which closes over the top of the windpipe during swallowing.

esophagus: the tube inside the body through which food goes down into the stomach.

ether: a colorless liquid with a strong smell. When you breathe it in, it can put you to sleep.

gas: a substance which is neither liquid nor solid. Air is made up of several gases.

germ: a tiny living thing that causes disease. Germs can only be seen with a very strong microscope.

gills: the part of a water animal which is used for breathing. Most animals with gills cannot breathe out of the water.

glottis: an opening at the top of the main breathing tube.

hay fever: the sneezing and watering of the eyes which happens to some people when they breathe in the tiny grains of pollen made by plants.

heart: the part of the body that acts as a pump to push the blood around your body.

hemoglobin: the substance which makes blood red. Hemoglobin carries oxygen.

hyperventilate: to overbreathe. We hyperventilate by taking a lot of short breaths. Sometimes, it happens when we panic.

infection: an invasion of part of the body by a germ, resulting in a disease. Measles is caused by an infection.

inflamed: to be swollen, hot, and sore.

larynx: the part of the throat used to make sounds.

lung: the part of the body which an animal uses for breathing.

microscope: an instrument that makes objects look a lot larger.

mucus: a clear, sticky substance which is produced by the lining of some parts of the body such as the nose and throat.

mucus membrane: a very thin, damp skin which lines parts of the body such as the nose and throat.

muscle: a material in the body which can move the bones to produce movement.

nerve: part of a network of tiny "cables" which pass messages from all parts of the body to the brain.

nitrogen: a gas found in living things and in the air around them. It has no color, smell, or taste. It does not burn.

nostril: one of the two openings in the nose.

organ: a part of the body which has a particular job, such as the brain or stomach.

oxygen: a gas found in air and water. Oxygen is very important to all plants and animals. We cannot breathe without oxygen.

pharynx: the top part of the tube which leads from the mouth towards the stomach; the throat.

pleural membrane: the thin, damp skin which surrounds each of the lungs.

pleurisy: a disease when the pleural membrane around the outside of the lungs becomes swollen.

pneumonia: a serious disease of the lungs during which the lung tissue becomes swollen.

pollen: the tiny grains of dust found in flowers. Pollen helps to make seeds.

pollution: something that dirties or poisons the air, land, or water, such as waste from factories.

red blood cell: a part of the blood which carries oxygen.

respiration: the way living things take in oxygen from air or water and use it to make energy.

respiratory center: part of the brain which controls breathing.

respiratory system: the parts of an animal which are used for breathing.

rib: one of the bones in your chest. Together, the ribs protect your heart and lungs.

rib cage: the group of bones in your chest which protects your heart and lungs.

sinus: a small space which is usually found in a part of your skull. There are sinuses in the bones of your skull near the nose.

smog: a poisonous mixture of smoke and fog, or fumes affected by sunlight.

spasm: a sudden, often painful, shortening of a muscle.

spiracle: one of the tiny breathing holes on the outside of an insect's body. Spiracles are joined to the tiny tubes inside the insect's body.

stethoscope: an instrument that a doctor uses to listen to sounds in your body made by parts like the heart, the lungs, and the stomach.

surgeon: a doctor who specializes in operating on the body.

tissue: when many cells of the same kind work together to do a particular job.

tonsils: two small lumps found at the back of the throat. The tonsils help us to fight disease.

trachea: the windpipe. The tube from the mouth and nose which takes air to the lungs.

transplant: when a part of the body which does not work properly is replaced with a healthy part from another person.

tuberculosis: a serious disease of the lungs during which lung tissue becomes covered with small lumps.

unconscious: to be unaware or not awake.

vaccination: giving someone a dose of specially-treated germs that are not strong enough to give the person the disease, but are just strong enough for the body to learn how to protect itself against the disease in the future.

vein: a tube that carries blood full of waste gases from all parts of the body back to the heart and lungs.

ventilator: a machine which pumps air in and out of a person's body through a tube attached to their lungs.

ventricle: one of two pumping chambers in the lower part of the heart.

vocal cords: the two thin bands found in the throat which vibrate when air passes over them. Your vocal cords control what your voice sounds like.

water vapor: water in the form of a gas.

white blood cells: a part of the blood that fights disease.

X-ray: an invisible ray that can be used to photograph some inner parts of the body from the outside.

Index